THE

PROMISE

IS STILL

VALID

THE

PROMISE

IS STILL

VALID

DR. BYRON J. WILLIAMS

CONTENTS

DEDICATION

This book is dedicated to the generations of whose shoulders I stand. My grandparents Marvin and Mary Williams, Ocie and Josephine Weeks, my loving parents Bennie and Ruby Williams. Although you were not here physically, I thought of you every day on this journey; I thank God for what you instilled in me. To the generation following after me, my daughter Kayla, my son Victor, my son-law Tim, and my granddaughter Sophia Joy. Thanks for allowing me to be your dad; I love you to the moon and back. You are always in my heart. To my New Beginning family, thank you for your support and prayers, for without both, I would have stopped this journey before it even got started.

FORWARD

G od made a Promise, in Jeremiah 29:11, to every one of us who loves God with all of our heart and soul; and, who loves his "neighbor" as he loves himself. God's statement in Jeremiah 29:1 (NIV) is the following: "For I know the plans I have for you, "declares the Lord", plans to prosper you, and not to harm you, plans to give you hope and a future." The question now is "has that Promise expired?" Is it dead?

Thank God that Dr. Byron Williams has stepped boldly forward to assert that "The Promise is Still Alive!!" This bold action by Dr. Williams to accept inspiration from God, and testify to us about God's promises and mighty works reminds me of a time in the Old Testament scripture where God told His Prophet to remind the Believers of the many terrible situations they had gone through; and, how God had come to their rescue each time. Now, God has directed Dr. Byron Williams, another one of His chosen Prophets, to teach us and remind us that His promises are still alive and well!

Dr. Williams is a unique and extraordinary person who has lived, navigated, and survived an extraordinary life! Through his sermons, personal ministry, and church leadership, he has been able to make a positive impact on thousands of people's lives; as well as, bringing salvation to hundreds of people's souls!

I am delighted to have been given this opportunity to comment on the life, character, and significance of the work and accomplishments of Dr. Williams. I first met him at a large multi-college recruitment showcase. He and I were competing for the same students to come to the separate colleges we were paid to represent. It is amazing how God works, how He interferes with our personal business. I am sure Saul felt the same way when God blinded him; and, told him where to go for further guidance. In like manner, at some time during that day, I was led to stroll over to his display table; and, quiz him about his total life. I wanted to know where he was from, what had been his career so far, what education he had so far, etc. I suspect that without God's influence on him, he probably would have rather harshly brushed me off. However, he told me that he was a U.S. Air Force Veteran (same as myself), was a laborer in Christian Ministry, along with other information provided. But he got into trouble with me when he said that he had not completed his college bachelor's degree as yet. I told him that the situation was totally unacceptable; and, that he must make the completion priority number one. I explained my college's Bachelor's completion program and convinced him to sign up for my program, promising to be his mentor forever. I wonder if God knew what He was getting me into!!

After Dr. Williams completed his Bachelor's Degree Program, continuing his commitment to excellence which led him to enroll immediately in my college's Master of Science in Organizational Leadership Program. He saw the Program as being very valuable for the leadership demands of his Christian Ministry. He was always striving to spread the Good News of Jesus Christ and lead his Flock, even while working full time and parenting a son. Yet, the story does not stop there! Dr. Williams contacted me and said that he wanted to pursue a Ph.D., a Doctoral Degree, while continuing to serve the members of his New Beginnings Ministry, working full time, and parenting his son. I told him that it would be extremely challenging; but, knowing the strength and drive of this great man of God, I gave him my blessings to proceed, believing myself that he also would receive God's blessing. Good news! At this time, he has completed all of the requirements to receive his Doctoral Degree, continuing to lead the New Beginning Ministry; and, now preparing to publish this book!

How blessed we all will be to read, learn from and apply the life lessons that he will share with us about how to keep the faith and fervently trust that God will always keep His Promises made to us. Yes, God's Promises alive, steadfast, and everlasting! Let's keep Dr. Williams and his book in our prayers. I can't wait to get my copy! And, I recommend that you get your own personal copy of Dr. Williams' book, emancipate your mind, unleash your energies, and achieve your destiny of success.

Prof. George C. Hairston
CEDO & Managing Partner, AI Optimize Solutions
www.ai-optimize.com

CHAPTER 1

What Was Designed To Kill You?

You know, at times in our lives, you may think you might not make it through the day, but we must believe God's love will keep us in what may seem to be the worst of times. We believe that He will not allow our homes to be damaged when the sump pumps stop working all of a sudden, but He will grant us His favor and mercy while believing He's going to bring us out of any situation, we may find ourselves. You have to believe that God has created you to do great things in your life!

"You have to believe that God has created you to do great things in your life!"

I recall this passage of scripture in **Daniel 3: 14-30.** It is a very familiar passage of scripture, in the sense that it is about three Hebrew boys - Shadrach, Meshach, and Abednego - and how they refuse to bow down to a false god. Many of us, at times in our lives, will be faced with the challenge of taking a stand for God, but we must be willing to trust Him no matter what comes our way. Sometimes taking a position will not be popular, but can you take a stand when things do not look good, when things do not feel good and when you are pressured? Can we still take a stand? Sometimes that even means taking a stand and minimizing yourself and not telling somebody off when you want to; when people get on your nerves, you really want to set them straight. It is something about how God will work things out for His people, and He will show you that His glory was manifested in the decision that you made not to do your own thing, but to trust in Him.

Let's Read The Passage:

14 *Nebuchadnezzar spoke, saying to them, "Is it true, Shadrach, Meshach, and Abed-Nego, that you do not serve my gods or worship the gold image which I have set up?*

15 *Now if you are ready at the time, you hear the sound of the horn, flute, harp, lyre, and psaltery, in symphony with all kinds of music, and you fall down and worship the image which I have made, good! But if you do not worship, you shall be cast immediately into the midst of a burning fiery furnace. And who is the God who will deliver you from my hands?"*

16 *Shadrach, Meshach, and Abed-Nego answered and said to the king, "O Nebuchadnezzar, we have no need to answer you in this matter.*

17 *If that is the case, our God whom we serve can deliver us from the burning fiery furnace, and He will deliver us from your hand, O king.*

18 *But if not, let it be known to you, O king, that we do not serve your gods, nor will we worship the gold image which you have set up."*

19 *Then Nebuchadnezzar was full of fury, and the expression on his face changed toward Shadrach, Meshach, and Abed-Nego. He spoke and commanded that they heat the furnace seven times more than it was usually melted.*

²⁰ *And he commanded certain mighty men of valor who were in his army to bind Shadrach, Meshach, and Abed-Nego, and cast them into the burning fiery furnace.*

²¹ *Then these men were bound in their coats, their trousers, their turbans, and their other garments, and were cast into the midst of the burning fiery furnace.*

²² *Therefore, because the king's command was [a]urgent, and the furnace exceedingly hot, the flame of the fire killed those men who took up Shadrach, Meshach, and Abed-Nego.*

²³ *And these three men, Shadrach, Meshach, and Abed-Nego, fell down bound into the midst of the burning fiery furnace.*

²⁴ *Then King Nebuchadnezzar was astonished, and he rose in haste and spoke, saying to his counselors, "Did we not cast three men bound into the midst of the fire?" They answered and said to the king, "True, O king."*

²⁵ *"Look!" he answered, "I see four men loose, walking in the midst of the fire; and they are not hurt, and the form of the fourth is like the Son of God."*

²⁶ *Then Nebuchadnezzar went near the [d]mouth of the burning fiery furnace and spoke, saying, "Shadrach, Meshach, and Abed-Nego, servants of the Most High God, come out, and come here." Then Shadrach, Meshach, and Abed-Nego came from the midst of the fire.*

²⁷ *And the satraps, administrators, governors, and the king's counselors gathered together, and they saw these men on whose bodies the fire had no power; the hair of their head was not singed nor were their garments affected, and the smell of fire was not on them.*

²⁸ *Nebuchadnezzar spoke, saying, "Blessed be the God of Shadrach, Meshach, and Abed-Nego, who sent His Angel[e] and delivered His*

servants who trusted in Him, and they have frustrated the king's word, and yielded their bodies, that they should not serve nor worship any god except their own God!

²⁹ *Therefore I make a decree that any people, nation, or language which speaks anything amiss against the God of Shadrach, Meshach, and Abed-Nego shall be cut in pieces, and their houses shall be made an ash heap; because there is no other God who can deliver like this."*

What was designed to kill you? Turn around the thing that was designed to kill you as the Lord turned it around on your behalf. Sometimes it's not necessarily a physical death, but you know you have people who may have tried to cut off your career or people who tried to tell you that you're not going to be anything, or situations may have come that God had to step in on your behalf. The one thing that Shadrach, Meshach, and Abednego have in common that we should model ourselves after is that they did not allow the situation to sway their mind about the God that they were serving. Sometimes circumstances will come, and people will **press** and **test** you, but you cannot allow the situation to change your mind about the God you serve.

> *"Sometimes circumstances will come, and people will* **press** *and* **test** *you, but you cannot allow the situation to change your mind about the God you serve."*

When you have people in your ear that don't mean you any good, and they have their own agenda, you have to be careful and ask God to show you the people that are in your corner. The people that are not in your corner will whisper in your ear and try to set you up for failure. So, the boys got into a situation where they were set up by the king, and the king did not realize it. Sometimes your enemy does not even understand that they are being used for the glory of God. The king had no idea that at this point he was going to be used for the glory of God. So again, we see how God can take a situation that seems like it is out of control and turn it around in our favor.

"Sometimes your enemy does not even understand that they are being used for the glory of God."

The king made a decree that when people heard music, they had to bow down to worship no matter where they were, no matter what time of the day was. They had to bow down and worship. However, the king made a deal with Daniel and the boys, making them exempt from that decree. What he found out was people were coming in talking to him, telling him about the Hebrew boys. The message to the king was, these three young men refuse to bow down and all of a sudden, the king was backed into a corner. He said to himself, "I've told people they all have to bow down and now I have this group of people who are not. I have to save face." You do not have to save face as long as you stay with God.

God will keep you in a place where (as long as you remain humble and serve him) you will be held in a safe place where you don't have to make a deal or compromise with people. We see here that when we fast forward through the story to the time and place where the music was being played, the king ordered the Hebrew boys to come to him. When in his presence, he said to them, "I need you to bow down. I understand what the agreement was, but you need to bow down with the music." The Hebrew boys acknowledged the decree, but they stated they would not bow down because we serve someone greater. We have to be that confident in our relationship with God that when the enemy comes, we are able to say, "No matter the test, I serve someone greater." Sometimes you will be called out and you will need the boldness and strength to stand. God will instill in you the courage to stand no matter what you are facing. Sometimes, you may become weak in your body, or you may become ineffective in your spirit, it is then you will have to trust the Holy Ghost and lean on God to get you through.

"When the enemy comes, we just have to say, "No matter the test, I serve someone greater."

Sometimes you may go through situations, that make you physically ill to the point that all you are able to do is rely on God. In my experience, when I was under a physical attack in my body, like the Hebrew boys I had to stand on the promise of God. If this is your story, know that you are going to have to make a declaration over yourself and believe that if God allowed it, then God will get you through it. So, the Hebrew boys were wise enough to know that this is the God that they serve, therefore they did not care about the situation; they didn't care how hot the furnace was, because they believed God would protect them.

At this point, the three Hebrew boys had enough confidence in their relationship with God that nothing was going to shake their faith. The decision was made at this point by the three Hebrew boys to display confidence that the God they serve would make a way of escape. Sometimes you have to let your enemy know and say, "Take your best shot!" Do what you think is best for your existence, but I serve a God that is going to keep me strong, and when the dust settles, I will be standing with the victory!"

> *"Sometimes you have to let your enemy know and say, Take your best shot! Do what you think is best for your existence, but I serve a God that is going to keep me strong, and when the dust settles, I'm still standing here with the victory!"*

The king commanded the furnace to be exceedingly hot, as he wanted to make an example of the Hebrew boys for their disobedience to the decree. In spite of their fear of the furnace, they stood there and said, "Do whatever you have to do." They did not fight. They did not run. They just stood there waiting for the king to take his best shot. The King's men prepared them to be placed in the furnace, but it was the King's men who ended up dying.

This is how God works in that your enemy will set you up for failure but will end up facing failure themselves. Sometimes your enemy will try to use you to make a statement on their behalf but what they do not realize is that their planned demise is a set up for

THE PROMISE IS STILL VALID

God's glory. <u>Have you ever had a situation where your enemy tried to set you up and somehow the thing that they designed for your downfall turns around, and it becomes their downfall?</u> Whatever has been intended to kill you will need to take a backseat to your faith in God. Your current reality may seem overwhelming, but as long as you trust God you will triumph over whatever challenges you may be facing. As long as you stand and believe in God, the thing that was designed for your failure will work out for your good.

> *"As long as you stand and believe in God, the thing that was designed for your failure will work out for your good."*

God has a way of doing things that will leave your naysayers speechless, causing them to wonder, "If God will do this for them, surely I need to serve a God like that." There are also times that people will try to hinder the gift that is inside of you. Not because they do not like you but because they see the presence of God operating in your life. You have to keep walking and standing with full assurance in your relationship with God. Quitting is not an option as you must continue to move forward in order to fulfill God's promises in your life. In spite of what was designed to take you off course the distractions will not work. *Can you remember a time in your life when you wanted to give up and throw in the towel, and God reminded you of the promises that He has for you?*

When the hard issues of life appear right before your very eyes, you can rest assured that God will be right by your side. You do not have to complain about your circumstance or allow your mind to begin to play tricks on you. You do not have to say anything if you are a child of God because the God that you serve specializes in working things out on your behalf. He takes what seems to be the hardest moments in our lives and turns them into a God moment. That is His specialty.

That is where He gets enjoyment and pleasure: in working things, out on your behalf. All you have to do is stand firm in your <u>faith</u> and allow God to do the heavy lifting. We just have to show up. Sometimes fighting back can make a situation worse, and it can take away what glory God has for your circumstance, messing up the glory moment for the nonbeliever's opportunity to witness God's game changing power.

"The God that you serve specializes in working things out on your behalf. He takes what seems to be the hardest moments in our lives and turns them into a God moment. That is His specialty."

At times we will need to understand the value in keeping our mouth closed. There are times where God just wants us to <u>**be quiet**</u> and <u>**be still**</u>. God will allow somebody to speak on your behalf, bringing clarity to your situation. You have to remember people are going to be people, but God is always going to be God. That is what we have to understand in all situations. If we take away that glory moment from God, then we are no better than the naysayers. We have to let God do what He's going to do. We have to understand that God is preparing us for success. Our part is to *show up, be faithful, be consistent,* and *believe* that God has an expected end for His plan in our lives. When people see the victorious moments that have happened in your life, it will draw people to inquire about the God that you serve. People are going to ask, "How do you keep your faith? How do you keep going? How do you keep the circumstances under control? How do you not quit? How do you keep believing in God when your situation is jacked up? It is because of God. When you cannot sleep at night and you want to give up and give in to what was designed to kill you, God is saying, "No, not today!" God will not allow you to come into a situation if He does not give you the grace to stand. You have to take a stand for yourself. You have to take a stand for your children and your children's children. Every now and then you may have to stand in the gap for loved ones that need a breakthrough and are unable to stand for themselves.

"You have to remember people are going to be people, but God is always going to be God."

As God is working in your circumstance, it may seem you have been abandoned by Him to those looking from the outside. God has a plan to be so great in your life that will exceed the expectation that others have for you. God places you in situations in order for others to see how great He is, and to recognize His excellence in your life. When people think you are living a wonderful life, they do not see the sacrifices that you have made. They do not see the prayers and the tears that you have cried but only the end result. So, do not take it personally when are going through some of the worst times of your life and it seems as though no one understands. So many times, some of us, as Christians, want to quit and say, "Nope, I'm not doing this thing anymore," but God says, "Listen, I have to allow you to go through so I can draw people to me so they can see the glory of God that is in your life." Again, don't take it personally, because God has purpose in your life.

We have to be consistent in our walk with Him. When we are consistent, we allow the blessings of God to show up and speak life into the situation. Your enemy will have to acknowledge that the God that you serve will work things out on your behalf. God sees and understands when nobody else wants to be in your corner and they walk away from you. He is sending angels because he made a promise to you that He will come to your rescue and speak life at the very moment you need it most. You have to be confident in your relationship with God to stand and trust in His word. When you think you have lost it all, God has a plan to restore not only the things you lost but he can restore your hope as well. At times we can lose something that seems like a great loss, but the Lord will provide a harvest that will be seven times greater.

"When you think you have lost it all, God has a plan to restore not only the things you lost but he can restore your hope as well."

Not only does God want to restore our hope, but His word provides healing to any problem we are facing today. Whatever was designed to kill you cannot prosper against you because there is no weapon formed that is going to flourish. It does not matter how people may twist the truth, how many people may try to misguide you, or how many people try to set you up, the weapons are not going to prosper against you. As we have witnessed in the lives of prominent African American's such as Martin Luther King, John Lewis, Rosa Parks and many others, the position that you take can cost you your life, but your purpose will bring hope to others. Even as the enemy attempted to negate the purpose in the lives of Emmett Till, George Floyd, Breonna Taylor, and the list goes on; what was meant for harm, God turned it around used it for His purpose to impact change for the lives of His people. God cares enough about you and your household to do the same for you. He cares enough about you and your community. God cares enough about you and your destiny; he will allow the blessings to overtake your household.

> *"Whatever was designed to kill you cannot prosper against you because there is no weapon formed that is going to flourish."*

Remember that God is preparing His glory to be revealed in your life and we must be willing to accept where He may take us. His plan may not always seem fair, but God is always faithful to His word and to His promises. Just as he did with the three Hebrew boys who found themselves in a situation that was designed to kill them, God stepped in to terminate the purpose the enemy had for their lives thus revealing His true purpose. As believers in Christ, we must understand the situations we go through are opportunities for God to impact changes in the lives of others. That is why we can't quit. That is why we can't become complacent and forget about the purpose that God has for our life. So, do not worry about what you have to go through, just be prepared to trust God and His plan for your life. What you go through may not necessarily have anything to do with you because you love God and you trust God. It may very well be for the people that are watching your life and do not believe what your God can do. No matter what your circumstance, you will be victorious so when you come out of this thing, they will know that God is true, and He is faithful to His promises!

CHAPTER 2

Do Not Allow Your Past To Kill Your Courage

Have you ever been in that place where you know God is working some things out, but you still really cannot believe it is happening? Have you ever been in a place where you still have to find yourself trusting God? You may know all the particulars, you may see where you're going, but you always find yourself in a place where you still have to trust God. Even with the well-executed plan presented to Pharaoh for the children of Israel release from Egypt, Moses and the children of Israel still had to trust God. Even though at times it seems like there may be confusion going on in your life, you still find the need to trust God.

Deuteronomy 31:6-8 is God's reminder that while you are going through some of the worst times in your life, be strong and of good courage as He will be with you.

Let us Read The Passage:

6 *Be strong and of good courage, do not fear nor be afraid of them; for the Lord your God, He is the one who goes with you. He will not leave you nor forsake you."*

7 *Then Moses called Joshua and said to him in the sight of all Israel, "Be strong and of good courage, for you must go with these people to the land which the Lord has sworn to their fathers to give them, and you shall cause them to inherit it.*

8 *And the Lord, He is the one who goes before you. He will be with you; He will not leave you nor forsake you; do not fear nor be dismayed."*

Do not allow your past to kill your courage to move forward. Familiarity can kill you and your spirit of expectation if you allow yourself to become comfortable in a situation where God has not designed for you to be. You can stagnate your growth because you were not able to understand God's design for your life and move in what God has intended for you. The past can leave you feeling that you are not qualified to receive the promises of God.

Your past has a way of speaking to your self-confidence, which could lead to you not fulfilling all of God's purpose in your life. Some of the things that you have been through in prior years may, in time, have shaken your courage. Some of the things you have gone through in your past, may have you questioning your purpose and your destiny. <u>Do you wonder if you are where you are supposed to be, or if you are operating in your purpose?</u> You may be in the middle of questioning your destiny and you find yourself asking God "What is the delay in my purpose? God why is it not moving fast enough?" At times when we question God about our purpose, we can miss opportunities to fulfill the purpose He has for us. Our uncertainty and our actions can bring us to the place where we have to go back through the process again. Taking matters into our own hands or even returning to behaviors from our past can cause major setbacks in our walk with God. Don't question God's timing and do not allow the enemy to instill fear causing you to believe that God's promises will not be fulfilled in your life. "So what God is saying to you is do not allow your past to kill your courage but recognize that your past was necessary in developing the person that you are becoming in God." Stand strong and be strong and of good courage.

"Do not allow your past to kill your courage
but recognize that your past was necessary in
developing the person that you are becoming in God."

It is so essential that in your walk with God, you remember who you are and the value of your relationship with Christ. Sometimes, the cares of this world will attempt to change your character and try to have you forget, about who you are and whose you are! You have a victory that you just have to understand belongs to you regardless of what your past might have indicated.

When you look back at your whole life, you may wonder "How in the world did I survive those moments where I believed I was not going to survive physically or emotionally. How did I survive spiritually when I wanted to give up on God? How did I survive life's challenges that tried to alter my relationship with God? How did I survive that divorce? How did I survive not having a job? How did I survive the frustration of not completing a goal?" God has placed in you the courage and the ability to overcome life's pressures and make the believer that He wants you to be." Regardless of what you see, God is still working out the plan for your life. Our daily walk with God, serves as a reminder that He will be with us through the hard times in our lives. We are reminded that his love for us will not fail and that He is committed to our success. God is committed to developing your courage regardless of what you are going through and He will not abandon you during this process.

> *"We are reminded that God's love for us will not fail and that He is committed to our success."*

Our past may have caused us to feel that our goals were unachievable, and we may have lost hope in the plans for our lives, but God comes to remind us that our plans are not over. He is in the background orchestrating a succession plan from our past failures and setbacks. You cannot allow our past to kill your courage as God is reminding you that He did not bring you to this point in life to forsake you. God does not specialize in quitting. The Lord will send you a reminder of how great your purpose is in life. We all have a purpose regardless of where we find ourselves. As a child of God, you have purpose. If you are claiming to be a child of God, you have purpose. Your purpose is relevant as long as you understand that God has placed the courage inside of you and gives you the strength to keep showing up. You have everything you need to keep moving forward.

"Your purpose is relevant as long as you understand that God has placed the courage inside of you and gives you the strength to keep showing up."

Be of good courage, fear not, and be not afraid. All of that sometimes comes as a challenge in our daily walk as human beings. If we try to walk this walk as human beings and forget about the strength that God provides for us, we can be left feeling inadequate leaving the door open for past issues to come back and cause us to stumble. We don't want to return back to those days where wanted to stay in the house and stay in the bed with the covers over our head, but we want to fulfill all the promises that God has for our lives. You cannot be in fear about the next steps God has for your life and you cannot fear the process that He has you going through right now, but we must embrace the courage that He has developed in us. Can you imagine the children of Israel when they left Egypt someone saying, "I'm going back? I will go. I am going back to bondage. I'm going back." But then others said, "We have to keep going. Even though we don't know what's out there."

Don't allow your past to keep you from moving forward, even as people will attempt to remind you of the person you used to be. These are the times that God's courage will remind you that you have a better future. As you come in contact with people from your past DO NOT BE DISTRACTED. This can be a trap by the enemy to pull you back into the person you once were. People from your past can try to divert you from completing the plan that God has for your life. It is not that you do not love or care for them, but in this season of your life God is preparing you for greater. With that being said, if God has freed you, God has delivered you then trust Him enough to LEAVE IT ALONE.

As you are following the path that God has set for you, you cannot be afraid or fearful of leaving your past behind to trust God with your future. It may be uncomfortable; it may not look good, and no, it may not feel good, however God will be with you and will not allow you to fail.

God will instill in you the ability to encourage yourself, just as He did with David in 1 Samuel, chapter 30. After becoming greatly distressed in verse 6, David had to find the ability to encourage himself in order to hear a word from the Lord. Taking a moment to listen to the voice of God, during stressful times in our lives can prove to be the difference between us being successful or losing what God intended for us to have. In this passage of scripture David received permission from God to recover everything that was lost. Here is where we will see the benefits in having a solid relationship with God. It shows that even during times of stress and worrying you can still hear the voice of God giving us clarity and direction as we move forward in the plan that he has for our lives.

"The ability to hear the voice of God brings clarity and direction as we move forward in the plan He has for our lives."

As much as we desire an encouraging word from our peers, our spiritual leaders, or people that we admire, the best place to receive an encouraging word during times of uncertainty is from a relationship with God. <u>Have you ever experienced a time where you thought you could get some encouraging words from somebody, and they just do not hit the mark?</u> God's desire is to not allow your past to kill your courage, but that you grow from past experiences in order to achieve the promises that He has for your life. It is essential in our relationship with God to hear his voice and embrace the courage He has given us to receive the victories that He has already provided for us. That is why it is so important to have courage.

The challenges in our lives, at times, will leave us seeking answers from God, but the one thing that we can count on is that God has provided us new mercies. The mistakes that you have made in your past, we oftentimes wish we can take things back or hit the reset button, but God gives us the courage to see those mistakes as opportunities to grow into the person that God is calling us to be. We serve a God who has already spoken into your future existence prosperity and well-being. Have the courage to move in God's plan for your life and don't get stuck in your past."

CHAPTER 3

After You Have Suffered
For A While

G ive all your worries and your cares to God for He cares for you. Stay alert. Watch out for your great enemy, the devil he prowls around like a roaring lion looking for someone to devour—stand firm against him. Be strong in your faith. In his kindness, God calls you to share his eternal glory by means of Christ Jesus. So, after you have suffered a little while, He will restore, support, and strengthen you, and He will place you on a firm foundation. All power to him forever. You are going to make it.

1 Peter 5:6-11 says *at the right time, God will lift you up.* Not in our time you know that God's time is always so much better than our time.

Let us Read The Passage:

6 *So humble yourselves under the mighty power of God, that he may exalt you in due time:*

7 *Casting all your care upon him; for he careth for you.*

8 *Be sober, be vigilant; because your adversary the devil, as a roaring lion, walketh about seeking whom he may devour:*

⁹ Whom resist stedfast in the faith, knowing that the same afflictions are accomplished in your brethren that are in the world.

¹⁰ But the God of all grace, who hath called us unto his eternal glory by Christ Jesus, after that ye have suffered a while, make you perfect, stablish, strengthen, settle you.

¹¹ To him be glory and dominion for ever and ever. Amen.

Nobody likes to suffer or deal with complicated issues in their life and because we try to avoid suffering, we end up doing things that will cause us to suffer more. You end up making mistakes and making decisions based on an attempt to avert suffering, and sometimes you end up going through worse than what you should. For example, your doctor may recommend certain things for you not to eat but you choose to eat those things anyway. This may be counterproductive to your doctor's instructions and can result in undue suffering. This is what I mean, because we don't like to suffer, we end up making mistakes or making choices that causes our own demise. Like it says in 1Peter 5:6, humbling yourself to the mighty hand of God in due time, He will position you to withstand the suffering. Just as following the doctor's orders can bring you healthy results in due time.

Sometimes, there are things that we go through that we do not have to go through because we do not humble ourselves under the mighty hand of God. Everything that you want to do is not always good for you. God says he wants you to humble yourself at the right time. That is the thing, you have to understand that at the right time, God is going to move things on your behalf, and sometimes waiting for the right time can be difficult, especially when you have to go through tests and trials alone. Waiting for God's timing to be active in your life can be challenging, especially when it seems like all hell is breaking loose, but it is during these times when God is birthing a powerful anointing out of your suffering. You are not going through just because God just likes to pick on you, but you are going through because God is trying to complete something in you. God is preparing you for an amazing and anointed time that is going to be life changing.

> *"Waiting for God's timing to be active in your life can be challenging, especially when it seems like all hell is breaking loose, but it is during these times when God is birthing a powerful anointing out of your suffering."*

It is going to be something that is going to blow your mind. The people around you are not going to understand what is going on, but there is an amazing anointing that God is trying to birth out of you. When the Bible tells you that He cares for you, it also says that at the right time; He's going to lift you up. He also reminds you to watch out for the enemy. You have to watch out for the haters. You have to watch out for the naysayers. You have to watch out for the people that pretend to be close to you but see the anointing that God is placing on your life. When God begins to move in your life, you would be surprised how many people will be upset and jealous.

The enemy can even see greatness in you; and that's why at times the enemy will come to assassinate your character and assassinate your emotions in an attempt to devour you at the crossroads of your breakthrough and your anointing. The enemy can see the greatness of God working on the inside of you so even while you are suffering you will experience people walking out of your life in the midst of your suffering. So, don't worry about that divorce; you will heal. Don't worry about the friends that walked out on; you will recover and stand stronger than ever. After you have suffered a while, the Lord will strengthen you, and bring clarity for your purpose and plans that He has for your life. The beautiful thing about God's plan for your life, is that He covers you while you're suffering. God has a way to cover you that people around you will not even know that you're suffering. God has a way to bring hope in the middle of suffering. There will be times you feel like crying and breaking down, or even quitting, but God has you covered. God has the ability to strengthen your faith in order to complete the goal that He has for your life. Stand firm against the enemy and be strong in your faith.

You must be mindful not to abandon your faith in God, nor lose sight of your purpose. At times you have be careful not to have more faith in our own capabilities, more faith in our finances, education or our life experiences that we lose sight of our faith in God. You have to remember to stay affirming your faith even at times you may feel alone as there are believers all over the world who are going through similar life experiences. Don't be more focused on the pain that we miss the importance of what God is preparing for us. The greatness that is in you at times is visible to everyone except you.

> **"The greatness that is in you at times is visible to everyone except you."**

The reason why the enemy wants to stop you in your tracks and the reason why he wants you to focus more on your suffering than the destiny that God has for your life is that he wants you to quit. He wants you to give in to the ideas of your past failures. He wants you to give in to the thoughts that remind you that you were never going to be successful. He wants you to give in to the fact that people have left you broken but the grace of God is not designed for you to quit at the moment of your breakthrough. The devil was an angel in heaven at one point and has the power to look forward into your future, but he does not have to power to alter your destiny unless he gets permission from God.

When God tested Job, the enemy had to get permission to touch Job's body as the devil cannot do more than what God allowed him to do. When you are going through some of the worst times in your life you have to remember that the Lord is not going to put more on you than what you can handle. The God that we serve is in the business of blessing you through your suffering. He is not in the business of seeing you defeated or seeing you lose your mind. God is in the business of seeing you come out victorious as the grace of God leads you to the glory that God had designed for your life.

God is birthing new attitudes and new characteristics out of your suffering. In other words, for you to experience growth in your walk with God, there will be a need for some attitude adjustments in your life. The suffering that you experience will cause you to develop new characteristics as you build on your Christ-like mentality. If Christ had to endure suffering for us despite the miracles that He performed, and regardless of the lives He saved, then surely, we understand the suffering we endure is just for a little while.

The pain that Christ endured was to get the attention of the naysayers and nonbelievers.

Suffering is intended to get your attention. The reason why your attitude must change is that if you go through your moments of suffering with the wrong approach, you'll miss out on the plan that God has for your life. Changing our attitude towards praising God will be essential if you are going to be victorious, as the wrong attitude can extend your suffering. If you trust in God, your personality, your attitude, and your character can change through your suffering. In your walk with God don't allow your suffering to push you away from what God has already done in your life.

"Changing our attitude towards praising God will be essential if you are going to be victorious, as the wrong attitude can extend your suffering."

During our times of suffering, we must remember that it's the grace of God that covers our old self until the new version that God is creating in us becomes triumphant. It's even in these moments that God is making us better as His grace is still actively working on our behalf. That is why it is so important that we still worship God, that we still continue to trust His word, and that we continue to have faith that he will bless us even in our suffering. It is essential that we activate our faith through our prayer and worship daily.

The suffering comes to build a firm foundation in your relationship with God. Your suffering is not for naught. Do not be in a season where you miss what God has for you. He has some great things in store for the believer, but it is going to be at the right time. Humble yourself and God will open up the doors of opportunity for you. "That is why we must see our suffering as a way to perfect our walk with God. This is essential to our spiritual growth."

CHAPTER 4

Yesterday Was Good, But My Tomorrow Will Be Better

At the time of the death of Moses, Joshua became the new leader for the children of Israel. As the new leader Joshua had to remind the people that the same God that was with them yesterday under Moses will be the same God that will be with them on tomorrow. Sometimes we find ourselves reflecting on yesteryears thinking about how good those days were. This chapter comes as a reminder to us that no matter how good yesterday was our God has a plan to make our tomorrow even better. Sometimes not knowing what the future holds can challenge our faith walk, but God provided directions in Joshua chapter 1:6-9 that tells us to "Be strong and of good courage and you will inherit the promises of God for your life."

Joshua 1:6-9 6. "Be strong and of a good courage: for unto this people shalt thou divide for an inheritance the land, which I sware unto their fathers to give them."

Let's Read the Passage:

⁶ *Be strong and of a good courage: for unto this people shalt thou divide for an inheritance the land, which I sware unto their fathers to give them.*

7 *Only be thou strong and very courageous, that thou mayest observe to do according to all the law, which Moses my servant commanded thee: turn not from it to the right hand or to the left, that thou mayest prosper withersoever thou goest.*

8 *This book of the law shall not depart out of thy mouth; but thou shalt meditate therein day and night, that thou mayest observe to do according to all that is written therein: for then thou shalt make thy way prosperous, and then thou shalt have good success.*

9 *Have not I commanded thee? Be strong and of a good courage; be not afraid, neither be thou dismayed: for the Lord thy God is with thee whithersoever thou goest.*

Joshua 1:9 says, "*Have not I commanded thee, be strong and of good courage. Be not afraid, neither be thou dismayed: for the Lord, thy God is with thee wherever thou go.*" Joshua said to the people, "Sanctify yourselves for tomorrow. The Lord will do wonders amongst you." You have to get ready to move. As you prepare to transition from your yesterday to your tomorrow, you may find yourself wanting to hold on to your yesterday. God has a better tomorrow for you than your yesterday. You just have to be willing to let go of your past and trust God with your future. When Joshua spoke and told the people to sanctify yourself for tomorrow, he was telling them to prepare for new opportunities that God was going to create in their lives.

Many times, God wants to do new and exciting things in our lives, but we have not prepared our mindset to receive God's blessings for our lives. Sometimes we want to hold on to the past but this passage in Joshua says to us as believers we have to prepare to go after what God has for us. We can't get stuck on what may have happened to us in the past. We can't worry about how we're going to get to what God has for us, we just have to prepare to move in His timing and not our timing.

> *"We can't worry about how we're going to get to what God has for us, we just have to prepare to move in His timing and not our timing."*

Waiting for God's timing will require us to develop courage in our faith walk with God, which means we cannot be worried or allow our past to keep us from the tomorrow that God has planned for us. Moving in God's timing will allow you to overcome your fears of what people think about you. So many times, we have missed God's moving in our lives because we were more concerned about pleasing people than pleasing God. Joshua reminded the people in verse 8, the value in meditating on the word of God and the peace God's word can bring to your life. God does not want us to panic as we leave our yesterday behind but in fact, He wants us to accept what yesterday was while preparing for His glory to take place in our tomorrow. For some of us, there is some hurt, and pain associated with our yesterday and God sees and understands your struggle. God stands ready to bless you in your tomorrow if you are willing to trust him today.

> *"God stands ready to bless you in your tomorrow if you are willing to trust him today."*

As you grow in your relationship with God, you will learn how to believe in your own destiny. You may have been told that you were destined to fail, but the Bible says that you were created in His image, and because you were created in His image, you are not destined to fail. You may have struggled in your yesterday and even while reading this book, you feel like you have let God down, but he did not create you to be a failure in life. The key to our successful tomorrow is having the courage to let go of our yesterday and believe that God has our tomorrow in his hands.

As you learn to trust God with your tomorrow, you may not have all the details, but you have to believe God is preparing you for a glory moment. When God was preparing the children of Israel, the glory moment was not where they were, but it was designed to where they were going. In our walk with God, we must be prepared to move when God says move in order for us to experience His glory in our lives. God has all the details already worked out for our tomorrow, but it is up to us to have faith in His plan for our lives.

Your tomorrow is going to require you to have faith, faith in knowing that God has not brought you this far without a plan. Your tomorrow is going to be better, and God is doing some extraordinary things in your life right now. One of the things that Joshua instructed the people to do was to gather their things and prepare to change their location. In other words, he was preparing them for the shift that was about to take place in their lives. God wants to shift some of us right now but because we are stuck in yesterday, we cannot receive the promises that God has for us. There is a new season that God has destined for us, but we have to be prepared to shift our way of thinking today for our tomorrow to be better.

The children of Israel were freed from bondage and at this moment in the scriptures, they felt pretty good about where they were. Like some of us in our lives today, we may feel pretty good about where we are today, but God wants to do some new and exciting things in our lives. We thank God for our yesterday because he's done so many things for us, but now let us prepare our hearts and minds for our tomorrow because has prepared us to receive new benefits. God has not run out of miracles. He stands ready to bless you in your tomorrow.

CHAPTER 5

Cast Your Cares Upon Him

God cares about you and your struggles so much that He challenges us to give Him our concerns to release us from our daily burdens. As we daily seek God, His desire is for us to walk in our purpose and fulfill the plan that He has for our life. God has a purpose in stepping in on our behalf, to take our burdens away so that we can live a victorious life. As we mature in our relationship with God, one thing that we can always count on is Him being present in our lives.

Psalms 55:22 says, "Cast your burden on the Lord, and he shall sustain thee: he shall never suffer the righteous to be moved.

Let's Read the Passage:

18 *He hath delivered my soul in peace from the battle that was against me: for there were many with me.*

19 *God shall hear, and afflict them, even he that abideth of old. Selah. Because they have no changes, therefore they fear not God.*

20 *He hath put forth his hands against such as be at peace with him: he hath broken his covenant.*

21 *The words of his mouth were smoother than butter, but war was in his heart: his words were softer than oil, yet were they drawn swords.*

²² *Cast thy burden upon the Lord, and he shall sustain thee: he shall never suffer the righteous to be moved.*

God is not going to allow the pressure of life to overtake you, life may push you, but it is not going to overtake you. In fact, the pressure God has you under is designed to push you into your destiny while preparing for the realm of where you're supposed to be. God shall sustain you; He shall never permit the righteous to be moved." So why are you worried about how things are going to work out for you in your life? He did not design us to be stressed out nor will He allow the enemy to overtake. He is going to give you the strength to go through, no matter the circumstance in your life.

God will give you the strength to stand up and be counted while He provides you with the strength to survive your storm. Will he cover you and provide you with the ability to escape through the storm? God will give you peace when chaos is closing in all around you. Have you ever been in a situation where God's peace has sustained you? As you learn to cast your cares upon Him, you will see that God will not allow you to lose your mind and that his grace will prevent the idea of you giving up.

No matter what is going on around you, God is going to sustain you, and He will never allow you to be moved. He is not going to allow failure in your journey as He enables us to fulfill the destiny He has placed on our lives. You have to be willing to cast your cares on Him, turn it completely over to Him, and leave it there. Do not take back the burden but learn to let Him take care of it. God specializes in taking your burdens and turning them into joyful moments. You matter to Him.

After you develop a relationship with God, you will learn the importance of rejoicing in the midst of your stressing. The value that we have in our relationships with Him is that while we turn our cares over to him, we can begin to rejoice in the victory that He has already prepared for us. Our praise that we have offered up to Him during our times of struggle has already started to manifest victories the moment we turned it over to Him. Our yesterday worship experience is the reason why some of us are receiving blessings today. Casting your cares upon him develops the courage in you to continue pressing, worshipping and honoring Him.

"Our praise that we have offered up to Him during our times of struggle has already started to manifest victories the moment we turned it over to Him."

Whatever you are going through that may seem to be frustrating you today, just know that God is in the plan. You do not need to know all the details and you may not know all the answers to your questions but just know that God will work it out for you. Like a kid at Christmas time, you were excited to see whatever blessings your parents left for you under the tree. You did not ask any questions. You were not concerned about how many hours of overtime your parents had to work; you were just excited about your Christmas joy. The same way in our walk with

God, when he begins to open the doors of the season of blessings in your life, just like our parents, God wants our expression of gratitude. Even though you may not see the full manifestation, He has done things behind closed doors that you do not know about. He's going to walk you into a season of favor.

God is making you in this season to prepare you for the next season that is coming in your life. And you thought your breakthrough was not happening. I am crazy enough to believe that God is going to work things out in my life because, with God, failure is not an option. Do not be afraid of your setbacks because it is a set up by God to get you to the next level of victory. Just like winter sets up spring, spring set up summer and summer sets up fall, trusting God prepares you for the upcoming season in your life. As you prepare to walk into your Wealthy Place, don't be ashamed of your blessings when God brings you out. You have been tested and tried, paying the price for your blessing and because of your perseverance, you have been proven faithful in the eyes of God and He will reward you.

"You have been tested and tried, paying the price for your blessing and because of your perseverance, you have been proven faithful in the eyes of God and He will reward you."

CHAPTER 6

This Is Not The End Of Your Story

There are times in our daily walk that we have to remind ourselves that I do not look like my story. For some of us our stories that were scripted by others in our lives were intended for us not to reap the full blessings of God. Even as the naysayers started forming around you, God began making a way of escape for you before you realized that there was a problem. He already started formulating a plan of victory by ordering your steps even before you even knew that there was a situation. Situations in our life come as a reminder that it is through our faith walk; this is not the end of your story.

Genesis chapter 22:1-15 speaks about Abraham and Isaac, but we will focus on Isaac and what God was doing in Isaac's life at this moment. Genesis 22:8 says, "And Abraham said, My son, God will provide himself a lamb for a burnt offering: so they went both of them together."

Let's Read the Passage:

¹ And it came to pass after these things, that God did tempt Abraham, and said unto him, Abraham: and he said, Behold, here I am.

2 *And he said, Take now thy son, thine only son Isaac, whom thou lovest, and get thee into the land of Moriah; and offer him there for a burnt offering upon one of the mountains which I will tell thee of.*

3 *And Abraham rose up early in the morning, and saddled his ass, and took two of his young men with him, and Isaac his son, and clave the wood for the burnt offering, and rose up, and went unto the place of which God had told him.*

4 *Then on the third day Abraham lifted up his eyes, and saw the place afar off.*

5 *And Abraham said unto his young men, Abide ye here with the ass; and I and the lad will go yonder and worship, and come again to you.*

6 *And Abraham took the wood of the burnt offering and laid it upon Isaac his son; and he took the fire in his hand, and a knife; and they went both of them together.*

7 *And Isaac spake unto Abraham his father, and said, My father: and he said, Here am I, my son. And he said, Behold the fire and the wood: but where is the lamb for a burnt offering?*

8 *And Abraham said, My son, God will provide himself a lamb for a burnt offering: so they went both of them together.*

9 *And they came to the place which God had told him of; and Abraham built an altar there, and laid the wood in order, and bound Isaac his son, and laid him on the altar upon the wood.*

10 *And Abraham stretched forth his hand and took the knife to slay his son.*

11 *And the angel of the Lord called unto him out of heaven, and said, Abraham, Abraham: and he said, Here am I.*

12 *And he said, Lay not thine hand upon the lad, neither do thou anything unto him: for now I know that thou fearest God, seeing thou hast not withheld thy son, thine only son from me.*

13 *And Abraham lifted up his eyes, and looked, and behold behind him a ram caught in a thicket by his horns: and Abraham went and took the ram, and offered him up for a burnt offering in the stead of his son.*

14 *And Abraham called the name of that place Jehovah Jireh: as it is said to this day, In the mount of the Lord it shall be seen.*

15 *And the angel of the Lord called unto Abraham out of heaven the second time,*

God began making a way of escape for you before you realized that there was a problem. He was already working on your behalf, by working out your plans for victory and ordering your steps even before you even knew that there was a situation. Circumstances come to remind us that in our faith walk this will not be the end of our story.

Even at that time Abraham was proven to be a prophet when he spoke the words," me and the lad, we will go worship, and we will come back again." Abraham received directions from the Lord, that he and Isaac would go and worship and be blessed in the presence of God. It is at this moment that Isaac's faith was being tested as he journeyed with his father Abraham. Abraham's faith was also tested as he learned during this journey that he would have to sacrifice his son. In our relationship with God, there may be times where we will lose or give up something that really matters to us. At that moment, we may honestly feel that this is the end of our story but as we mature in our relationship with God, we will realize that He is testing our level of trust in Him.

In this story, Abraham understood that having an agenda that is outside of God's plan would have caused Abraham to fail this test. What we can take from this is if we lose our faith in God, and act on our own agenda will we can fail our own tests and miss what God has planned for our lives. We cannot allow our disobedience, to cause us to miss out on some of the biggest blessings that He has for us. We have to walk in faith regardless of what people say or how things may seem. You do not have to be worried about the outcome when you operate in faith because in the end you <u>WIN</u>. You do not have to lose sleep nor continue to worry about how it is going to work out, just rest in your faith and confidence in God.

> *"You do not have to be worried about the outcome*
> *when you operate in faith because in the end you*
> *<u>WIN</u>."*

In our life's journey, the Lord will provide everything that you will need when we need it. Isaac spoke to Abraham, his father, I see the wood for the fire, but where is the lamb for the Burnt offering? Abraham stated; "My son God will provide himself a lamb for a burnt offering." Abraham and his son Isaac continued to the place which God had prepared for them. Abraham built an altar there. He laid the wood as instructed and bound up his son Isaac and laid him on the altar for sacrifice. As Abraham stretched forth his hand and took the knife to slay his son the angel of the Lord called out to him from heaven. The angel told Abraham to do no harm to his son for God provided a ram for the sacrifice. From this story we've learned that God will provide for us if we just have faith.

Abraham activated his faith when he spoke the word and said, the Lord will provide. Some of us find ourselves in the same situation as Abraham where we are going to have to speak life to our faith. Especially in moments where our faith is being tested on another level, one we couldn't even imagine. The Lord will give us clarity, knowledge, and wisdom in order for us to receive total success in our stories.

Abraham's moment of faith set in motion for God to do more for him in his life. God wants to do so much more in our lives because He loves and cares for us while concerned about our future. God is excited about you because He understands your story will impact more people than you realize. Your obedience and faith depend on each other for your future success. No matter your age or what you've been through, you still have a future and a purpose in God.

Your faith is critical to your relationship with God; it allows you to be available when God needs you. Every time the Lord called Abraham, he made himself available. Abraham's obedience to the voice of God did not end Isaac's story as a sacrifice on the altar. Sometimes when the Lord calls us, we have to ask, are we always available when he needs us? It is imperative that we obey God's voice as He is preparing for us to help someone else in their faith walk. Abraham's obedience to God served as a bridge to Isaac's faith in the Genesis chapter 22. Isaac's faith was stretched when he realized that he would be the sacrifice. Instead of abandoning the moment that God was preparing for him, he found rest in the words his father said to him, "The Lord will provide."' How many times have we abandoned God in the middle of our faith walk simply because we did not understand God's plan? We need to develop enough faith in God that we do not abandon our story prematurely. Our faith is an essential element for our story to be written. Your confidence allows the promises of God to be useful in your life. Without your faith, the life story that God has prepared for you cannot be written.

> "Without your faith, the life story that God has
> prepared for you cannot be written."

As your relationship with God matures, you will understand that listening to Him, regardless of what you see, _can_ and _will_ bring value to your life. I do not want you to miss the blessings that God has intended for your life. Your faith in God prepares you to be in the front row of your blessings that He has activated in your life. In moving forward, let us not allow doubt, fear, stress, or worries cause you not to trust God because this is not the end of your story.

CHAPTER 7

The Promise Is Still Valid

As a believer in God, one thing that we can be sure of that if God has prepared a promise for you, he will make provisions for you to reach your destiny. Just know that in whatever situation you find yourself in, God is going to meet you on the other side of it. He has already placed everything in motion that you are going to need for your journey. All He wants to know is can you trust him? Can we get in the boat of life and unconditionally trust God?

Matthew 14:31 says, "And immediately Jesus stretched forth his hand, and caught him, and said unto him, O thou of little faith, wherefore didst thou doubt?"

Let's Read the Passage:

22 *And straightway Jesus constrained his disciples to get into a ship, and to go before him unto the other side, while he sent the multitudes away.*

23 *And when he had sent the multitudes away, he went up into a mountain apart to pray: and when the evening was come, he was there alone.*

24 *But the ship was now in the midst of the sea, tossed with waves: for the wind was contrary.*

²⁵ *And in the fourth watch of the night Jesus went unto them, walking on the sea.*

²⁶ *And when the disciples saw him walking on the sea, they were troubled, saying, It is a spirit; and they cried out for fear.*

²⁷ *But straightway Jesus spake unto them, saying, Be of good cheer; it is I; be not afraid.*

²⁸ *And Peter answered him and said, Lord, if it be thou, bid me come unto thee on the water.*

²⁹ *And he said, Come. And when Peter was come down out of the ship, he walked on the water, to go to Jesus.*

³⁰ *But when he saw the wind boisterous, he was afraid; and beginning to sink, he cried, saying, Lord, save me.*

³¹ *And immediately Jesus stretched forth his hand, and caught him, and said unto him, O thou of little faith, wherefore didst thou doubt?*

³² *And when they were come into the ship, the wind ceased.*

In Matthew 14th chapter verse 22, immediately, Jesus made the disciples get into the boat to go ahead of him to the other side while he dismissed the crowd. When you start studying this passage of scripture when you understand this is the first time that the Lord sent the disciples ahead of him since he gathered them together. Since this is the first time the disciples were separated from Jesus, I'm sure it crossed their mind wondering where they were going without him. Even though at times we may feel that the Lord may not be right next to us he made a promise that he will always be there for us.

You may be feeling that the mistakes you made in life may disqualify you from the promises that the Lord has made in your life. We may have found ourselves in circumstances that were not worthy of God's love but because he cares about us, he did not allow the situation to cause you to miss the blessings for your life. When he made the selection of the disciples, the promise was secure, and at that moment, God knew there were issues in their lives. Peter was a disciple of Jesus and at the time he was selected by him Peter was a mess. Even though Peter was a curser, a fighter, a liar, and he denied Christ in the garden, Jesus still chose Peter. Just as some of us today with all of our hang-ups, our bad attitudes, and negative outlook on life, Christ still chose us.

Let's look at the example of Judas, one of the twelve disciples who was a liar, and betrayed Jesus, but he was still selected by Christ. Although we fall short in our faith in God, He still plans to fulfil the promises in our lives not because of where we were, but because of where we are going. In Matthew 14:28, Peter says, "Lord, if it's you bid me come." And the Lord says, "Come. Come out here. Come on, I have you. Just come." There are times in our lives when the Lord will ask you to come into new territories, new ideas, new businesses, or new ministries. At this moment when God is asking you to come, He has set no prerequisites other than to trust His word. Jesus did not ask Peter to get his shoes or his raincoat, Christ only requirement for Peter was to have faith. Many of us like Peter have heard the Lord say come but our lack of faith has made us too afraid to get out and trust God. Jesus just said come. And so, when Peter got out of the boat and began to walk on water with Jesus for that moment, Peter was at peace, but Peter allowed the distractions of the wind, the waves and the rain to lose sight of God's presence in his life. When God needs us to come, don't allow the distractions to cause you to miss what God has for your life.

"Although we fall short in our faith in God,
He still plans to fulfil the promises in our lives not
because of where we were, but because of
where we are going."

In our walk with God, we will experience distractions, but our faith is the key to successfully navigate through those distractions. Distractions can come in the form of people, our health, our finances, or the mindset of just wanting to do better. As these distractions come, we may lose sight of the plan that God has for our life but do not allow the distractions to take you off course from what God has for you. God is not going to abandon you because you became distracted. Even though Peter became distracted and began to sink he still had the mindset to ask for Christ help. Peter did not allow his pride to keep him from seeking the help at the time when he needed it the most. Like some of us, we really need to reach out and ask for God's help and as a reminder he is willing to lend us a helping hand.

God made a promise in the book of Hebrews chapter 6 verses 13 through 15 when God made a promise; he could swear by no one greater, so he swore by himself. God made a promise to himself to fulfill the destiny in your life. Do we define how God is going to help us when we ask for it? When you are stepping out on the promises of God, you can trust him more than you trust your circumstances which you can see. The Lord loves you too much to allow you to fail. His love for you is centered on the victory that he has planned for your life, so we must be willing to trust Him to receive the blessings that he has for us. Let nothing distract you from the purpose and destiny that God has for your life. When God speaks and tells you to come out, go, do not worry about these distractions. Do not worry about what is around the corner or what is next. Embrace the love that God has for you and love the fact that His promises are still valid and working in your life.

CHAPTER 8

New Beginnings

Here you can write your new beginnings; this chapter is left blank intentionally for you to be the author of your own story. May God bless you on this journey of new beginnings....

ABOUT THE AUTHOR

D r. Byron J. Williams was born to Pastor Bennie and Ruby Williams, in Fort Wayne, Indiana. He is the eldest of three children. His childhood reared in The Way of Holiness Church of God in Christ; Dr. Williams had a Bible-based upbringing that would later serve as the foundation for his transition into ministry. Upon graduating from high school in 1984, he attended Franklin College in Franklin, Indiana, and, subsequently, joined the United States Air Force in February of 1987.

In April of 1998, Dr. Williams acknowledged his calling in the Word ministry as a member of the Refreshing Spring Church of God in Christ and became an ordained preacher of the Gospel in August 2004 under the late prelate of the Washington DC Jurisdiction of the Church of God in Christ, Bishop Sherman S. Howard. Pastor Williams currently serves under the leadership of Bishop Melvin Robinson, Jr. of the Master's Child Church Worship Center in Indian Head, Maryland.

Since joining the Air Force, Pastor Williams has completed degrees in Personnel Management, with the Community College of the Air Force, Bachelor of Arts in Pastoral Studies from Southwestern College, a Master's in Organizational Leadership from Nyack College and a Doctoral degree in Business Administration with Capella University. After 22 years of service to the Air Force, Pastor Williams retired in March 2009.

After completing Clinical Pastoral Education training in 2009, Pastor Williams began serving as a Chaplain with National Rehabilitation Hospital Center in Washington, D.C. Pastor Williams served as a Family Advocate at Washington Hospital Center, where he provided grief and trauma counseling to patients, their families, and hospital staff and conducted bi-monthly worship services and spiritual care counseling. Today, Pastor Williams is employed as the Manager of DoD Programs with Oasis Systems of Lexington, Massachusetts.

On May 20, 2012, Dr. Williams opened the doors as Pastor and CEO of New Beginning Ministries in Suitland, MD, where he helps to direct and cultivate the spiritual life of students, parents, and the community through the Word of God. He is determined to be obedient to the call of God and to win souls for the Kingdom.

His message to the world is that Jesus lives, and Jesus cares about you, no matter your situation or problem, and lives by the motto: "Life isn't always fair, but God is always faithful."

Dr. Williams is the father to his beautiful children, daughter Kayla and son Victor, Son-in-Law Timothy, and his new sweetie pie granddaughter, Ms. Sophia Joy.

For More Information:

Visit our website: http://www.drbyronjwilliams.com

For More Information on New Beginnings Ministry

Visit our website: http://www.newbeginningmd.com

Made in the USA
Monee, IL
03 November 2020